...Story at 10

Coal-Worthy Holiday Behavior from the News

Caroline Tiger

STERLING INNOVATION
An imprint of Sterling Publishing Co., Inc.

New York / London
www.sterlingpublishing.com

STERLING, the Sterling logo, STERLING INNOVATION, and the Sterling
Innovation logo are registered trademarks of Sterling Publishing Co., Inc.

Library of Congress Cataloging-in-Publication Data

Tiger, Caroline.
  Santa arrested--story at 10 : coal-worthy holiday behavior from the news / by Caroline Tiger.
     p. cm.
  Includes bibliographical references and index.
  ISBN 978-1-4027-7005-0 (alk. paper)
  1. Crime--Humor. 2. Criminals--Humor. 3. Christmas-
-Humor. 4. Santa Claus--Humor. I. Title.
  PN6231.C73T54 2010
  818'.602080334--dc22
                    2010007832

10 9 8 7 6 5 4 3 2 1

Published by Sterling Publishing Co., Inc.
387 Park Avenue South, New York, NY 10016
© 2010 by Sterling Publishing Co., Inc.

Distributed in Canada by Sterling Publishing
c/o Canadian Manda Group, 165 Dufferin Street
Toronto, Ontario, Canada M6K 3H6
Distributed in the United Kingdom by GMC Distribution Services
Castle Place, 166 High Street, Lewes, East Sussex, England BN7 1XU
Distributed in Australia by Capricorn Link (Australia) Pty. Ltd.
P.O. Box 704, Windsor, NSW 2756, Australia

Design by Mike Rivilis
Photographs © Ben Asen

Sterling ISBN 978-1-4027-7005-0

For information about custom editions, special sales, premium and
corporate purchases, please contact Sterling Special Sales
Department at 800-805-5489 or specialsales@sterlingpublishing.com.

Contents

Introduction

The holidays are stressful times for adults and children alike. The anticipation, the preparations, the costs, the anxiety to get it all done right and on time ... Inevitably the pressure gets to some people and they react. Sometimes the response to yuletide tensions is tying on a few extra glasses of cheer, or it can manifest itself in the act of stealing the Baby Jesus out of a church's manger scene. Many people help themselves to another slice of pie, while others help themselves to sixteen tons of ham from a nearby warehouse. The point is, everyone reacts differently.

Here in *Santa Arrested* you'll read about the best of the worst people who have found themselves on Santa's naughty list. He sees you when you're sleeping, he knows when you're awake ... and he definitely finds out when you put lawn decorations in lewd positions and land yourself in the local paper! Every one of the merry misdemeanors in this book has been taken from real news articles around the world. A woman really did have her son arrested for opening his present early. The Health Department in Illinois really did give dozens of people food poisoning at its Christmas party. And a woman really did find a dead mouse when she broke open a Christmas cracker. You can't make this stuff up!

So the next time you're stressed out by Saint Nick and you feel like the holiday rush is just too much, read a page from *Santa Arrested* and pat yourself on the back for managing to keep yourself from incarceration this year.

Bad
Santa

Jingle Balls

A man dressed up as St. Nick decided to add his own twist to the traditional mall Santa. While walking through crowds of Christmas shoppers, he decided that dropping his pants would be a new and festive way to ring in the holidays. Luckily for the shoppers, he had red sweatpants on beneath his Santa pants. When mall security asked him to leave, he couldn't resist dropping his pants a few more times on his way out. Unfortunately for him, authorities still considered it indecent exposure and arrested the disrobing Santa. Does this mean he made it onto his own naughty list?

Nice Try, Saint Nick, if That Is, in Fact, Your Real Name

Oviedo, Florida
December 2008

Do people think that if they wear a Santa cap while committing a crime, their crime will be overlooked? Do they think the cap is akin to an invisibility cloak? Because, uh, it doesn't work that way. Two men in Oviedo, one garbed in a Santa beard and cap, found that out the hard way after a surveillance tape caught them trying to break into a store stocked with flat-screen televisions. The store owner had been the victim of thievery once before and had installed special security glass that thwarted Santa and his elf. The entire thing was caught on tape, and the owner let everyone know he was offering a $2,000 reward for catching the Santa impersonator and his helper.

Seeing Double Clauses

Norfolk, England
December 2000

Seeing your hero fall from grace can be a traumatic and life-changing experience. The children who saw Santa Claus get arrested and perp-walked by police at an annual holiday event in Norfolk were in tears when they realized Old Man Christmas was headed for the clink.

Santa is, of course, the star of this annual Christmas procession—he arrives in town on a sleigh to much fanfare. The crooked Santa was an extraneous Santa—he wasn't the feted Santa on the official sleigh—but kids can't tell the difference. To kids, each bloke with a white beard is special. When the other Santa got into a scuffle, authorities led him away and the kids' cheers and laughter turned quickly to wails of distress. They were so upset, the police took them on a field trip to the jail so they could see for themselves that the Santa who'd been arrested was not the "real" one.

Santa and His Sack of Morality

Knoxville, Tennessee
December 2008

S anta, the protester. It's a new role for Old Saint Nick, but the fellow pulled it off when he showed up at a board meeting for the CEOs of the Tennessee Valley Authority bearing stockings full of coal. The peaceful icon waited his turn, then schooled those CEOs about the harm their product does to his constituents, the children of Appalachia. The children couldn't go outside and play because of coal pollution, he told them. Many had seen their grandparents die, he continued, from asphyxiation.

Santa's not usually such a bummer! We're accustomed to seeing him spread joy and cheer. Not this time. He was eventually handcuffed and dragged away by police officers who were definitely not in the holiday spirit.

No, Santa!
Put Down the 40-oz!

San Francisco, California
December 1994

he "Bad Santa" movement got its start in 1994 when twenty-five men decided to rent cheap Santa suits and walk the streets of San Francisco while drinking beer from Pine-Sol bottles, staging Santa lynchings, singing naughty carols, and generally being loud and obnoxious. Perhaps it was an attempt to protest the commercialization of Christmas. Perhaps it was just twenty-five men looking to have a loud, good time. For whatever reason, there were fifty of them the next year, and things got out of hand. During a rampage through a department store, several items were stolen and several Santas arrested for behaving in an "un-Christmas-like fashion." The following years saw the annual event move to Portland, Oregon, and Los Angeles, California, and by 2008 there were nearly eighty copycat events around the real and virtual worlds, from South Korea to Sweden to Second Life.

Unless You Came Here in a Flying Sleigh, Get the Hell Out

Pittsburgh, Pennsylvania
September 2007

An intoxicated Pittsburgh man who was trying to surprise his girlfriend by sliding down her chimney got wedged inside and couldn't get out. He told a local television station, "I wanted to feel like Santa Claus." His girlfriend, who'd been dating him for eight months, was not amused by her boyfriend's drunken antics. "I've dated a lot of psychos in my life, but none like that," she told the newspaper. She stood in front of the fireplace so the firefighters couldn't break through the wall to save the man wedged inside. Her main concern: saving the bricks. Many of those bricks and lots of debris and dust ended up in a pile in the middle of her living room, and her boyfriend ended up out the door. According to the local paper, she pushed him out, throwing beer bottles and screaming at him never to return.

Not Your Typical Santa

Hollywood, California
December 2007

It's bad enough having to look at Borat in a G-string. The last thing you want to see is Jolly Old Saint Nick showing off yards of flesh. But that's what bystanders outside Grauman's Chinese Theater had to endure one December day when they saw police arresting a man wearing a Santa cap, a purple G-string, a wig, a red lace camisole, and black leg warmers. Contrary to what you might think, he wasn't arrested for indecent exposure, but for drunk driving. The deputy chief of police told the local paper, "We are pretty sure this is not the real Santa Claus." Only in Hollywood . . .

A Non-Traditional
Stocking Stuffer

Louisville, Kentucky
September 2009

All I want for Christmas is my two front teeth . . . and an AK-47? That was the case in Louisville, at least for one barbershop owner who launched a giveaway for an AK-47 valued at $750 to one lucky customer just in time for Christmas. As a lifetime member of the NRA, the barbershop owner decided to up the luck of fellow NRA members: the one-ticket-per-customer limit was lifted for NRA members, who could claim two tickets. For joining the NRA, he'd give you six tickets. His intent—and his true gift to his community—beyond arming a lucky someone with a semi-automatic weapon? Raising awareness about gun rights, of course.

Homeless for the Holidays?
Santa to the Rescue!

Miami Beach, Florida
December 1982

An officer in the Miami Beach police department who was on the homeless beat decided to put a little holiday spirit into his work by dressing up like Santa for his holiday arrests. Charged with arresting homeless people every day, he wanted to give his regulars "a little cheer, a little chuckle." He knows the homeless people in his precinct by their first names. He knows they'll probably spend Christmas on the streets. "These people don't even know that Saturday is Christmas. They don't even know what day it is," he told the local paper. Once arrested, they'd be taken to the county jail where they would be given a meal, clean clothes, and medical treatment when needed.

He approached each one with a "Merry Christmas," and his partner chimed in, informing them, "I'm Rudolph."

Imagine Going through Customs with Saint Nick!

Ottawa, Ontario, Canada
December 2008

Finally, Father Christmas can rest easily. Thanks to the Canadian city of Ottawa, which declared Santa a citizen in December of 2008, Old Saint Nick doesn't have to worry about being stopped at the border on his way home after a long, long night delivering presents. He now has full re-entry rights, and if he were ever to get frostbite or a fireplace-induced burn, he'd be covered by Canada's universal health care. The politician who made the announcement shrewdly noted that Santa's red and white ensemble matches the Canadian flag's colors. Even though no country can claim the North Pole as a territory, Santa apparently is showing his true colors in his outfit.

The strangest part of the whole thing was why it took Canada so long to make Santa a citizen. After all, their North American Aerospace Defense Command Santa tracker has been tracking his worldwide annual journey for fifty years, and it always shows him setting out from Canada. Santa was not available for comment.

Say What!?

When Microsoft created an automated elf for kids to instant message on its Live Messenger contact list (northpole@live.com), they had no idea the elf's software made it capable of talking dirty. The idea was for the elf to ask children what they wanted for Christmas and to then respond accordingly. Microsoft was surprised to learn of a chat between some young girls in the UK and the elf that led to the mention of oral sex. Apparently the girls repeatedly asked the elf if he wanted to eat some pizza at which point he responded, "You want me to eat what?!? It's fun to talk about oral sex, but I want to chat about something else." When Microsoft learned of the dirty talk, they made some changes to the software but ultimately decided to take the elf off-line.

Tell Santa What You *Really* Want

Los Angeles, California
December 2006

Every day at 5 P.M. at the Beverly Center in downtown LA, hunky Santa takes over for jolly Santa. A young, lean Santa with bulging biceps makes his entrance in true LA style: in a red convertible and accompanied by sexy female helpers. When he arrives, he hands his keys over to the valet. The shopping center hoped that shoppers would sit on hottie Santa's lap and get excited about spending money. That worked in some cases, but not all: Many still prefer their Santas chubby and jolly. One shopper, who found the muscle-bound Santa especially jarring, exclaimed to a local reporter, "Is that fellow even wearing a shirt?"

Christmas
Mischief

These Reindeer Won't *Be Heading* Home for the Holidays

Edinburgh, Scotland
December 2000

Mere days after vandals attacked a pensioner's Christmas tree in Port Seton, a suburb of Edinburgh, more local troublemakers preyed on the annual Christmas display in the garden of a family that had, for three years, proudly displayed three four-foot-tall wooden figurines of Santa's reindeer—Rudolph, Prancer, and Dancer—that had been handcrafted locally. For three years, they decorated the deer with festive rope lights. For three years, the figures delighted the neighborhood children. Then vandals ruthlessly beheaded Rudolph and Prancer, showing mercy only to Dancer.

The owner of the display told the Edinburgh Evening News, "All the kids who love to see the display have been upset because they think Rudolph the red-nosed reindeer has been decapitated." Her own young daughters were devastated when they woke up to the shattered reindeer. Still, she left the wooden bits scattered around the yard to expose the vandals' shameful handiwork, turning the Christmas display, sadly, into a crime scene frozen in time.

Knocking Down Elves
Will Not Stand

Temecula, California
December 1995

When a California couple woke up to knocked-down lights and candy canes and elves sawed in half, they didn't sweat it. They opted not to report the damage to the police. But the authorities found out about the crime when they saw it in the newspaper and decided to launch an investigation. So did the family's friends, who played amateur detectives in their quest to spot the pickup truck allegedly used by the vandals. With all the publicity, the couple became well-known enough in the surrounding community that a letter from a sympathetic stranger reached their mailbox despite the envelope missing their street address. Soon two city councilpeople took up their cause, introducing a $1,000 reward for information leading to the arrest and conviction of the Christmas vandals. Another councilperson told a local paper, the *Press Enterprise*, that such a reward was unprecedented in Temecula. According to the *Press Enterprise*, the wife could only chuckle to herself about the big to-do over damage that cost only $100 and a day to fix, but the council members insisted the act was "heartbreaking" and a "travesty."

Cover Your Eyes, Frosty!

Marietta, Georgia
December 2008

Vandals laying into holiday decorations is, unfortunately, a relatively common occurrence. In Cincinnati in 2005, a pair of teenagers was arrested for attacking an inflatable snowman with a screwdriver. But the expanding practice reached a whole new level in Marietta, Georgia, when the vandals put some of the holiday figures in, *ahem*, compromising positions. That's right: reindeer in sexual positions. It's almost impossible for certain images not to pop into your head when you hear that phrase. Even worse, the ringleader of this particular group of vandals was someone in a position of authority in the town, someone who worked with kids—a coach for one of the town's middle schools. He was driving his own students around at night to aid in their mischief. One of the victims of the vandalism chased the group's truck, caught up with them, and asked the ringleader what he was thinking. He replied, according to the local paper, "It's just a bit of fun."

Getting into the Holiday Mood
Wink Wink

Richmond, Virginia
December 2006

If vandals were going to strike, they shouldn't have struck these people: a couple in Richmond who were so devoted to Christmas that they dressed their dog, Lucky the Christmas Dog, in lighted holiday jackets every year. They even trained the sixteen-year-old dog to greet people visiting their home as part of the town's annual Tacky Christmas Lights Tour. The couple had been on the list since 1995. One morning in 2006, the wife woke up, excited to see an item about Lucky in the local paper. When she opened the door to retrieve the paper, her husband heard a loud shriek. Their lawn had been vandalized in the worst way. Their new polar bear was broken and strewn across the yard. Even worse, the husband told the local paper, "They put deer on top of each other, 'doing it.'" All in all, they estimated $400 worth of damages to their holiday display. It was enough to turn off the husband from the tacky-lights business. He told the paper he felt ready to retire, but predicted his wife would talk him off the ledge. After all, his daughter's five-year-old dog was already well into training for his future as the next Christmas Dog.

Yuletide Vigilante

Baton Rouge, Louisiana
December 1994

Constant vandalism during the holidays can wear on a peaceful homeowner and turn him into a vigilante. This is what seemed to be happening in Baton Rouge after a quiet subdivision suffered for years at the hands of an army of thoughtless, reckless vandals.

One homeowner complained that the figures in his Nativity scene were turned around so they were facing the wrong way. The spotlights pointing toward his decorations were smashed. A neighbor's eighteen-foot-tall Christmas tree, strung with lights, was destroyed; it was the fourth act of vandalism that particular homeowner's holiday displays had suffered.

The homeowners guessed the ne'er-do-wells were neighborhood kids. The president of the homeowner's association told the local paper that he thought parents should be held responsible for their kids' criminal acts. Then he posted an ominous sign in his front yard where his Christmas tree once stood. It read, "Next year this Santa will be watching—and he won't be packing toys!"

This Is Why We Can't Have Nice Things

Ballater, Scotland

For decades, the lucky townsfolk of Ballater, in Scotland's northern Highlands, have enjoyed a holiday tradition: a gift of a beautiful evergreen from one of three local grand estates. One of those estates, Balmoral, happens to belong to none other than the Queen of England. The people of Ballater display the tree proudly on their Church Green. It's a sort of thank-you gift from the Royal Family, who source many products and services from Ballater's shops and businesspeople.

It was one thing when someone playing football on the Church Green damaged the lights on the tree—accidents are unfortunate, but they do happen. The year the vandals ripped out the power cables and smashed the lights— well, that was a different story. The lights cost Ballater Enhancement Group £800. And the attack was such that new lights could not be reconnected.

Was this an attack on the town? On the Royal Family? No one knew how to read it. In typical stiff-upper-lip fashion, the Enhancement Group's secretary told the local paper, "We are very disappointed."

Is Nothing Sacred?

Dubuque, Iowa
December 2000

Maybe it was all the excitement of the millennium. Maybe Mercury was in retrograde. For whatever reason, Dubuque's 2000 holiday season saw a rash of vandalism. Thieves broke the metal clamps on a UPS truck to break in and steal packages that probably held Christmas gifts for a number of soon-to-be-disappointed folks. Citizens' decorations were vandalized. Police stopped an SUV that matched witness descriptions of the vandals and found $150 worth of decorations inside. But the worst act of all was the theft of the Baby Jesus from the Nativity scene in the town's main square. When crowds gathered for the dedication, they discovered that the twenty-two-inch fiberglass figure was missing. Thieves had cut through the manger wires that were meant to protect the centerpiece of the Christmas scene and stolen the babe within.

How About a Pressed Ham
for Christmas Dinner?

Valentine, Nebraska
November 2008

According to a local paper, a radio station called him "the butt-cheek bandit." The bandit, who somehow kept eluding authorities, was approaching storefronts at night and pressing his butt up against windows and doors, leaving smears of Vaseline on the glass. As the incidents grew in number, it was thought that there might be copycat butt-cheek bandits. The town's police chief wondered aloud to the local paper, "Who in their right mind would do something like that?" Indeed. People will do crazy things around the holidays.

Something Worse than Coal in Your Stocking

Madison, Wisconsin
January 2008

Another heartwarming holiday story—well, at least it's a washing machine-warming story. What was going through the mind of a Wisconsin teen who was visiting the apartment building next to his own to poop in their laundry room? Specifically, he aimed his turds directly into the washing machines (it's unknown whether they were top or front loaders), ruining a comforter, baby clothes, and other garments. He was also charged with defecating in one woman's tennis shoes that she'd left outside her door. A police report quoted her as saying she "had not given anyone permission to defecate in her shoes and she was disturbed." Merry belated Christmas.

Assault with a Deflating Weapon

Cincinnati, Ohio
December 2006

After his inflatable Frosty the Snowman fell victim to two earlier attacks, one Ohio man decided he'd had enough. He didn't want to have to repair his Frosty a third time with white masking tape, as he'd had to do twice before. He was going to play vigilante. He told the local paper he was tired of asking, "Why me? And why Frosty?" So he set up a motion-sensitive video camera in his yard to catch red-handed any vandals who dared go after his snowman. Sure enough, two teens showed up one night with a screwdriver and proceeded to assault poor Frosty. The footage is brutal—the balloon sways and bows with each vicious jab. The teens had no idea they'd been caught on tape until police showed up at one of their homes. His accomplice soon turned himself in.

Santa Is Going to Be Pissed!

Panama City, Florida
December 2001

A young couple calling themselves atheists decided to express their views by defacing a church in Florida on Christmas Eve. Their vandalism consisted of writing satanic messages, including "666," "Devil rules," and "Lucifer," in marker on the church and the church van. They also slashed the van's tires. The tires had been slashed a few weeks earlier, and other satanic messages had been scrawled in ketchup. The church had spent $500 on new tires and would have to shell out the money again. The couple told police they wanted the churchgoers to see their messages when they arrived at church for Christmas morning services. They should've done their homework, because the church didn't have any services scheduled.

The Big Uneasy

There were lots of victims of holiday crime in New Orleans during the season of 1994: a three-foot plastic Frosty the Snowman lawn decoration that was kidnapped, devastating a six-year-old girl who coveted Frosty and considered him a member of the family; a woman whose illuminated snowman, Santa, and Santa's sled were stolen from her front lawn three hours after she set them up; and the citizens who enjoyed Lafreniere Park's holiday decorations, which were completely destroyed by vandals. The crime spree was so overwhelming, it prompted many others to bring their holiday decorations inside. "I want to put them up in my front lawn," one citizen told the local paper, "but I'm afraid." Santa would clearly be skipping New Orleans that year.

Frankincense, Myrrh, and a GPS

Bal Harbour, Florida
December 2007

I n yet another town plagued by an increase in theft of the Christ Child, a hardcore overseer of the town's Nativity scene became so adamant that Baby Jesus never be a victim again, she bought him a GPS. She did the same for the other main players: Mary and Joseph. "We may need to rely on technology to save our Savior," she told a reporter. One previous year, Jesus was bolted in place and vandals still figured out how to steal Him. As an extra measure of precaution, the supervisor also installed Plexiglas in front of the display.

The Ultimate Last Laugh

Ashland, Oregon
December 2007

Talk about a good gag: An Oregon man who was beloved for his sense of humor passed away in October of 2007 but still managed to send Christmas cards with a return address of "Heaven" to thirty-four of his closest friends two months later. The eighty-eight-year-old was working on the ploy for a decade with his accomplice, his barber. Over the years he frequently updated the mailing list and kept giving her more money to cover the rising postal rates. During a haircut in October, he looked up at her from the chair and told her she'd be able to mail them this year. He died a week later. The cards read in part, "I asked Big Guy if I could sneak back and send some cards. At first he said no; but at my insistence he finally said, 'Oh well, what the heaven, go ahead but don't (tarry) there.' Wish I could tell you about things here but words cannot explain." A friend for nearly twenty-five years told the paper, "It was just so [him], always wanting to get the last laugh."

Santa Is Not Amused

Missoula, Montana
December 2007

College students: They do the darnedest things. One twenty-two-year-old in Missoula thought it'd be funny to throw a pie in the face of a shopping mall Santa. He thought it would be so funny, he even filmed it for a short film he was pulling together on pranks and antics. When he arrived at the mall, he saw Santa was busy with a fifteen-year-old girl who was telling him what she wanted for Christmas. The prankster waited a few minutes for the girl to finish, but ultimately decided it would be funnier if she was on his lap. He walked up to Santa, smooshed a pumpkin pie in his face, and shouted, "What do you think of that, Santa?"

The prankster retreated and was lurking in a corridor, waiting to approach his victim to sign a film release, when the police caught up with him and made an arrest. "It's a good thing he didn't wait around longer," a police sergeant told the local newspaper, "because I think Santa would have laid him out."

Nut Jobs Roasting
on an Open Fire

Sometimes people get a craving that just can't be ignored. Such was the case with a man who got stuck in the chimney of a barbeque restaurant for more than eight hours, until a neighbor heard his cries for help. Firefighters yanked him up and out of the chimney—he had gotten stuck with his hands raised straight up and over his head, so they were able to get a good grip. When the man told authorities he'd been forced down the chimney by a lone gunman, they were dubious. He faced charges of attempted burglary until the owner of the restaurant opted not to press them, telling the local paper he'd talked to the probable-burglar on the phone and he seemed like a good kid. Besides, the incident was turning into a great promotional opportunity. The restaurant owner had T-shirts in mind: "What people won't do for J&E Barbecue."

Poor, Poor Rudolph

**South Shields, England
December 2007**

A drunken teen became the poster child for drinking-age advocates when he got liquored up and proceeded to ride—and severely damage—a decorative reindeer that had been erected only days earlier to bring holiday cheer to the small village of Whitburn. Perhaps it was a bad idea to place the reindeer, which cost a whopping £2,000 (over $3,300), outside the Jolly Sailor Pub, where hooligans began violating it as soon as it appeared. There was enough vandalism to merit the installation of a security camera, which is how the teen was pegged with causing the damage and received a warning from the police. Santa was probably none too happy, either.

The 120 Criminal Reports of Christmas

Hamilton, New Jersey
January 2008

Kids. They're supposed to be at home asleep on Christmas night, dreaming of sugarplums and sleighs. Instead, four teenagers in New Jersey were out on a vandalism spree that caused estimated damages of up to $50,000. In a car and armed with a metal pipe, the teens smashed car door mirrors, headlights, and windows over the course of three very destructive hours. Instead of enjoying a calm Christmas morning, police were deluged with phone calls from the many angry victims. The reports kept coming and coming until they numbered an unbelievable 120. What made the incidents even more unbelievable was that the kids were bright students with no prior history or records. It seems that they still had some important Yuletide messages to learn.

Christmas
Criminals

I Want a Football, a Toy Train, and a DNA Test

Barry Island, South Wales
December 2000

A window cleaner in South Wales was charged with a four-year-old crime when improved DNA techniques were able to trace a bloodstain near the smashed kitchen window of a burglarized home back to him. He broke into a home just before Christmas and stole £4,000 (about $6,500) worth of presents. He committed the crime, it was surmised in the local paper, not for himself, but to help out a friend who owed money to a drug dealer. Since the crime, he'd been contracted by the local magistrates court and city hall to clean their windows. It goes to show you never know who's really cleaning your windows, even if you're a governing agency.

Maybe You Should Ask Santa for Some Smarts

Oyster Bay, New York
December 2005

A forty-four-year-old man was arrested when he tried to return $2,198.93 worth of equipment— a desktop computer, an MP3 player, a digital camera, a 2.5-inch television, a home theater system, a phone, and a digital memory card—to a RadioShack on Long Island. The man claimed the booty was all Christmas gifts that he didn't want or need, and he asked for a full refund. However, he made two very big mistakes: 1. He didn't have a receipt, and 2. he tried to return the items to the very same store from which he'd stolen the stuff a week before. Employees recognized the man from when he'd loaded all of the above into his car and then driven off without paying. The crack employees called the police and humored the man until the authorities showed up at the shop and arrested him.

Half Holiday Merrymaker, Half Heartless Thief

Lewiston, Idaho
December 2008

The robber who stole a woman's wallet at a convenience store in a small town in Idaho probably didn't count on there being a surveillance video of the encounter. He definitely didn't count on a still from the video being published on the front page of the local paper. It must've been a slow news day, because that day the paper also published a nice, human-interest photo of a man painting Christmas messages on the front window of a local business. A newspaper editor's job is to read his paper closely, and one of the editors was doing his job that day when he peered at the photos and noticed the painter's resemblance to the wallet snatcher. The connection was pointed out to local police, who agreed and quickly arrested the multitasking thief.

A Real Mama's Boy

Deseret, Utah
December 2008

He just wanted to see his mother on Christmas. Unfortunately, he was in Utah, she was in Washington, and he had no ride. So the twenty-five-year-old mama's boy tried to steal a $500,000 fire truck. The firefighters couldn't help but notice they had a thief in their midst once he accidentally hit the horn on the big rig. The truck snatcher saw the firefighters coming, so he put the thing in reverse—and nearly sideswiped an ambulance. The chances he'd see his mother for Christmas? Not so good. When the firefighters tried to get their truck back, the desperate son put up a fight and a brawl ensued. Instead of sitting by the tree with Mum, it was looking like he'd be in the big house for Christmas.

The Case of the Stolen Santa

Mesick, Michigan
December 2002

It's a mighty big target, and it must've been difficult to steal without drawing attention to themselves: a one-hundred-pound, seven-foot Santa who sings "We Wish You a Merry Christmas." Still, someone managed to steal it less than a month before Christmas from outside The Red Barn in Mesick. Police deduced that it was a two-person job (one hundred pounds is just too heavy for one person). They found telltale tire tracks and beer bottle caps near the empty spot where Santa once stood and sang. Even with the store owner's offer of a $100 reward, no one was 'fessing up.

The Great Christmas Computer Caper

Gulfport, Mississippi
December 2005

Those computer repair places can take forever! And these days, it's hard to be without a computer. When you're not connected online, you can feel disconnected from life. No e-mail, no Skype, no Twitter—what's a person to do?

Around Christmas in 2005, a man in Mississippi was feeling particularly frustrated without his computer, so he broke into the computer store where he'd brought it for repairs to reclaim the machine. He was in the crawl space above the ceiling when the panels gave way beneath his weight and he fell, crashing onto several computers. (It's unknown whether one of those was his computer.) Needless to say, he was caught red-handed. According to the local paper, he told the police, "I don't see myself looking too good."

No Wonder Santa Doesn't Visit Him

Chevy Chase, Maryland
December 1997

He just wanted some Christmas presents. That's why the twenty-three-year-old man broke into a house early Christmas morning—but late enough to ensure Santa had made his drop. The owners of the house heard something downstairs and called 9-1-1. Police cars showed up and officers jumped out and ran into the house with their guns drawn. Despite all the ruckus, the burglar stayed sitting beneath the Christmas tree, happily ripping open wrapping paper.

A Different Kind of Santa

Minneapolis, Minnesota
Christmas 2003

A man stuck in a chimney on Christmas morning—you would think there was a good explanation for that. He was just trying to deliver toys, right? Sadly, that wasn't the case when a thirty-four-year-old man was found drunk and naked and stuck in the chimney of a Minneapolis bookstore on Christmas Day. He was not delivering toys, nor had he dropped his keys down the chimney and was trying to retrieve them, as he told local police. The bookstore's owner heard noises from the chimney when he came in that day to hang signs for the post-Christmas sale. He called the police, who extracted the man from the chimney, slapped a burglary charge on him, then took him to the hospital to treat his bruises and scrapes.

A Conspicuous Christmas Disguise

Lansing, Michigan
December 1998

A teen runaway and an elf costume—these are two separate entities that don't usually go together. But they did around the holidays in 1998, when a teenager was being tried at the local courthouse for breaking into and entering people's homes. He fled wearing his flimsy yellow prison uniform—not exactly enough to protect him from the cold winter air in Michigan. Luckily he found an elf costume in the trunk of the car where he sought refuge. The costume—an elf hat, green and red boots, pants, and a sweatshirt—was meant for an office party. It soon became the costume of a fugitive when he donned the ensemble for warmth. The car's owner returned and opened the trunk, forcing the teen to flee again, his elf hat bobbing as he ran. It wasn't too difficult for police officers to find and apprehend him.

Toys Not for Tots

New Smyrna Beach, Florida
December 1998

Toys for Tots is not synonymous with "Toys for the Children of the Charity's Seemingly Enthusiastic Coordinator." Unfortunately, this was the misunderstanding of a man in Florida, who for several years took on the job of soliciting donations of toys for the organization. The toys presumably went to poor children at Christmas, but instead of acting as the middleman, the coordinator brought the best toys home from the collection center to give to his own family. His son and his son's girlfriend also abused Toys for Tots—they sold the toys for profit. When their horseplay was discovered, all three were arrested.

A Lesson Well Learned

Shandong Province, China
January 2007

A Chinese schoolteacher approached a terrible situation with patience and an attitude infused with the holiday spirit: When her purse was snatched, she realized the thief was probably using her cell phone, so she began to send text messages to her own phone, pleading for her property to be returned. Her purse contained her bank cards and cash. The schoolteacher was persistent and continued to send up to twenty-one gently worded messages, even when she received no replies. The thief must've decided to speak through his or her actions instead, because the schoolteacher arrived home one day to a package at her door. She opened it to find her purse and all her belongings, plus a note that read, "I'm sorry . . . I'll correct my ways and be an upright person."

On Dasher, and Dancer, and Robbers, and Thieving

Vernon, British Columbia
January 2008

It was a very poorly planned bank robbery. So soon after Christmas—perhaps these small-time criminals were still in a holiday haze. Their first mistake: running down the battery in the getaway car. While Robber #1 was busy robbing the bank, his accomplice, Robber #2, was sitting in the car, playing the radio with the ignition off. The activity was just enough to drain the battery of its remaining juice. When Robber #1 fled the bank, he found the car empty. Robber #2 was in a nearby bakery, trying to call a cab. It didn't take long for police to find and arrest the robbers as the bank happened to be located in the same building as a police station. (Oh yeah, that was their second mistake.)

Sleigh Bells Ring
While You're Stealing

Anderson, Indiana
December 2007

eing a Salvation Army bell ringer is a noble deed around the holiday season. You have to stand outside in the cold, beseeching worried and harried shoppers to give a little more during a time when everyone feels a pull on their purse strings. It's no easy charge. In Indiana, one such bell ringer was apparently feeling a little entitled from doing his charitable work. When he went on a break, he entered the Wal-Mart where he was stationed. While inside, he slipped $20 worth of holiday ornaments inside his jacket and a fast-food takeout bag. Police reported he was singing "The First Noel" as he pilfered the goods. At least he was in the holiday spirit while he was ripping off the store!

Some Elves Just Left It Here, I Swear!

Missoula, Montana
November 2007

The owner of a Christmas shop in Montana called the police when he saw a man walk by with a cart full of wreath-making supplies he recognized as his own merchandise. The man was walking to his home, a few blocks from the store. Upon further investigation, the shop owner spotted two of his Christmas trees in the man's yard. The man hadn't even removed the shop's red and yellow sale tags. Still, the accused insisted a friend gave him the trees as gifts. As for the rest of the booty, he claimed he found them abandoned near the store.

Ho Ho, Oh No!

Redwood City, California
December 2001

One county caseworker was a little bit like Santa with his list of gifts intended for families in need. Unfortunately, he was a little like Satan once he had the gifts. A coworker tipped off authorities when he noticed his fellow employee loading bags of gifts into his gold Lexus sedan instead of delivering them to the Human Services building to be sorted and distributed to needy families. It turns out the man stole a total of forty gifts that had been donated in response to wish lists filled out by seven families from his own caseload. Instead of passing the gifts on to these families, he gave them to his own relatives. Judging by his car, they weren't even close to being part of his caseload.

And with a Better Selection than Macy's

Portland, Oregon
December 2007

W hat better time is there to rob a UPS shipping depot than Christmastime, the most wonderful time of the year? You're sure to find lots and lots of great new merchandise—holiday gifts being sent all over the country, to and from families and friends. That is, until they're intercepted by a wily thief.

That was the case in Portland, where a man broke into a UPS warehouse and stole around 280 packages that included, among many other items, a glow-in-the-dark puzzle, a toy dump truck and matching hardhat, and a Spiderman lamp. The thief was pretty picky, discarding a bunch of packages he didn't want at an apartment building. A resident in the building saw the packages, figured someone was up to no good, and notified UPS.

The Double Dirty Deed

Syracuse, New York
December 1998

If she had an employee discount, it clearly wasn't enough to satisfy. One sales clerk at a Bon-Ton, a chain department store that sells everything from clothing to cosmetics to sheets and towels, decided to give herself the old five-finger discount. The young woman "forgot" to charge her brother for nine pieces of clothing totaling almost $300, and she invented a fictional return in order to pocket nearly $120 in cash from the register. When her boss and the police caught on to her thieving ways on Christmas Eve, she confessed to stealing even more from her employer, including another $700 in bogus returns and letting a friend walk out with some clothing worth over $100.

Bellying Up to the Christmas Burglary Buffet

Oostburg, Wisconsin
January 2008

One Wisconsin teen celebrated Christmas a little late when he mistook one street in his town as "under the Christmas tree." He thought everything on that street—everything in the mailboxes and on people's porches and front yards—was for him. After he was caught by the police, the list of his spoils was revealed: a white T-shirt taken from a porch; a DVD box set of *The Johnny Carson Show* left outside a garage; an MP3 player, also left outside a garage; several Christmas cards taken from mailboxes (opened and discarded once he discovered they held no money); and magazines taken from the same mailboxes.

That Looks Like a Good One, Right There, Next to the Shopping Cart Corral

Providence, Rhode Island
December 2002

Modern-day society has become so detached from the early pioneer days of living close to nature that we sometimes make basic mistakes. Two men made such a mistake when they pulled their Jeep Cherokee up to a Super Stop & Shop shopping plaza and began cutting down a pine tree that was part of the plaza's landscaped grounds. Surely they knew this tree wasn't up for grabs? Maybe so, maybe not. Police assumed the worst and slapped the two with misdemeanor charges of malicious damage.

How Many!?

Chicago, Illinois
December 2006

Each year there are many thefts from Nativity scenes—the Baby Jesus is perhaps the most prized booty, followed closely by the Virgin Mary. But there are very few vandals who arrange their spoils as neatly and methodically as one Chicago thief, who managed to steal thirty-two Baby Jesus dolls from people's front yards, then line them up neatly along the fence outside one Chicago woman's home. When the homeowner found them, she turned them over to her parish priest.

An Unfortunate Office Party

Yonkers, New York
December 2006

Christmas brings out people's best—and, unfortunately, their worst. Perhaps it was a hatred of office parties, the holiday crunch on finances, or just a Grinch-like attitude that drove one person to the latter. In Yonkers, one thief stole $14,000 in staff bonuses and other funds from an office safe during a Christmas party. By the time he was caught, he'd already spent $7,500 in cash, but $6,500 in checks were returned to their rightful owners.

An Unlikely Grinch

**Flushing, New York
December 2006**

A twenty-five-year-old man was the main character in a Flushing, Queens, fiasco dubbed the "Christmas Day Caper," when he stole around $25,000 from a church's safe during their Christmas morning Mass. The man and an accomplice snuck in through a back door and were lugging the two-foot metal safe out of the Church of Saint Mel when someone saw them loading it into a Lincoln Navigator with Vermont plates and asked what they were doing. According to the *New York Times*, they replied they were removing some elevator equipment.

Once they arrived home, the man who owned the getaway vehicle called the police to report it stolen. Police already had an APB out on the SUV, and he was soon arrested at his home in Brooklyn. Neighbors were astonished. The man, they told a reporter, wore a suit and tie to work. He had a wife and kids. They never would've expected him to steal from a church on Christmas.

Wearing Your Holiday Best

**Essen, Germany
December 2007**

Technically, the three wise men were homeless, at least for a while. So they may not have minded a homeless man borrowing their robes and headdresses from a life-sized Nativity display near a Christmas market on a very cold winter night. The man undressed Caspar, Melchior, and Balthasar, piled the garments on, and went to sleep outside a department store on Saturday night. That's where security guards, surprised by such a richly attired homeless person, found him the next morning.

Cutting Christmas Costs
with Sticky Fingers

All Over the US
December 2008

A downturn in the economy always causes an up tick in petty crimes. That was the case in December 2008, when the US was at the beginning of what some would label the Great Recession. You didn't have to look at the Dow or the stock market to know—all you had to do was look at Christmas-tree sellers across the country. In Baytown, Texas; in Portland, Oregon; in Hillsborough County, Florida—more than twenty trees lifted by sticky fingers. Since there's little evidence of a black market for Christmas trees, it could only be assumed these thieves were filching the trees to hang their own ornaments on the branches. One Florida tree seller told a newspaper that the last time he'd seen such a trend was in 1978, during another bad economic time. He planned to install motion detectors and a night watchman for the rest of the holiday season.

Charitable Spirit Gone Awry

Grand Rapids, Michigan
December 2008

More tales from the Great Recession of 2008: In an astounding act of selfishness, a woman stole toys that were donated to the Salvation Army to give to needy children during the holiday season. When her bail was set for $10,000, she had the nerve to turn around and ask the judge for $10,000. When times are tough, people will try anything for a buck.

That's a Lot of Ornaments!

Raynham, Massachusetts
December 2008

Christmas trees aren't the only item targeted for theft during the holiday season. Even thieves consider the holidays a time for creating a festive, inviting home filled with Christmas cheer. Unfortunately, they can't always pay for it. That's why one garden center near Boston found that its stock was lighter the day after someone stole $1,500 worth of table runners, Victorian ornaments, and tabletop arrangements from their shelves. And if that weren't enough, a few days later someone took a $120, fourteen-foot fir tree. How to catch a thief? Look for the home with the nicest holiday decorations.

A Modern Day Robin Hood . . .
Sort Of

Philadelphia, Pennsylvania
December 1999

The typical kid doesn't have to wonder whether his Christmas gift fell off a truck. But that's what some needy kids were dealing with a few days after a holiday party at a Philadelphia homeless shelter where forty-four Raleigh bikes were doled out by a reputed mob boss dressed up as Santa. Soon after, the boss and thirteen of his associates were charged in a $1.3 million interstate theft and drug ring. The list of stolen merchandise in the indictments included 618 Compaq computers, 240 Sony TVs, 1,101 Samsung TV-VCRs, 1,000 ceiling fans, 570 Raleigh bikes, and 15,500 women's sweat suits. The US Attorney told the local paper there was no way to know whether the Raleighs distributed at the shelter were hot.

Lifting Grandma's Holiday Spirits

Mesa, Arizona
December 2008

It's probably not a good idea to cover your car's license plate with a piece of cardboard—this could prompt some suspicion. Case in point: When an officer spotted a Ford Crown Victoria parked at a Shell gas station with its license plate shrouded, the cop became curious and discovered the car matched one that was wanted in a recent nearby alcohol theft from a Circle K. Police followed the car to a home where a large holiday party was taking place. One of the teens in the car fled into the crowd, but the cops chased and arrested him. In the end, all three teens in the car were arrested and two confessed to the theft. Here's another good idea: When grandma sends you on a beer run during a holiday party, pay for the stuff.

It's a Giveaway, Not a Takeaway

Pawtucket, Rhode Island
December 2001

Staffers at the Boys & Girls Club were shocked when they went to the room where they were storing toys for their annual holiday giveaway—and the room was empty! One hundred seventy-five toys were gone. Someone had broken into the club and stolen the gifts—piles of games, puzzles, dolls, robots, and all manner of toys that'd been donated and collected over many weeks. They were meant for 250 needy children from the city who were looking forward to an afternoon of food, games, and a visit from Santa Claus. The party was just two days away. Amazingly, when reports of the crime got out via radio and television news, gifts started pouring in. An incredulous worker for the Boys & Girls Club told the local newspaper, "When it's all done, we may wind up having more gifts."

They Must Have Had Brass Christmas Balls

**Miami, Florida
December 2006**

Who'd ever think that a van parked outside the Police Benevolent Association and locked with a padlock would be at risk? This is where firefighters in Miami were storing $5,000 worth of gifts meant for an annual holiday party for children with cancer. More than four hundred children were due to congregate in Miami Beach for a holiday party that was only a few days away. The firefighters had spent weeks collecting, wrapping, and sorting the toys. When the captain went to check on them the Monday before the party, he found the padlock broken and the van empty. The thieves had also stolen $500 worth of tools meant for hurricane cleanup. Don't you wonder who those "toys" were for?

The Finer Things to Swipe

All Over France
December 2004

In France, the holidays are called *les fêtes*, which translates literally to "the feasts" or "the big parties." Not much of a difference between France and America: We both like to party big-time around December and January. We have something else in common, too: a habitual rise in shoplifting right before the holiday season.

In 2004, a UK newspaper reported that, though French police were prepared for the up tick in armed robbery that always occurs the month prior to les fêtes, they had never before seen so much poaching of luxury food items. That year there was a rash of bandits with very sophisticated tastes: One man in southwest France got eight months in prison for stealing eighteen tons of oysters—on moonless nights, he and his gang would steer a boat out into the aquatic oyster farms and pluck baskets straight from the sea. Other poachers around the country robbed foie gras warehouses, dug up truffles, and broke into trucks transporting bottles of bubbly. Leave it to the French to have thieves with acquired tastes.

Not Your Normal
Stocking Stuffer

Hull, England
December 2002

T he citizens of Hull banded together around the holidays in 2002 to fight crime. In their bid to prevent a repeat of 2001—when, from November to January, thieves on the hunt for Christmas booty broke into two thousand cars around town—a local organization passed out ten thousand "crime prevention packs." Each pack contained a sign for people to post inside their cars to warn burglars the cars were locked, fully alarmed, and contained no valuables. The city passed out more than enough packs so locals could share them with friends and loved ones. After all, there's no better way to say "I love you" than to say it with a crime prevention pack.

A Return for the Holidays

Oklahoma City, Oklahoma
December 2002

What a great scam: Steal something from a store, come back a few days later, claim you lost the receipt, and get the full price plus tax on the item you pilfered. Called "return fraud," it's something that happens country- and worldwide every holiday season. In 2002, retailers expected to lose $3.5 billion on this particular type of fraudulent behavior, according to the National Retail Federation Foundation. Most of the thievery is an inside operation, with store employees collaborating with friends and colleagues in crime—and the stores aren't the only ones losing money to the criminals. Thank this unscrupulous group for the higher prices you're paying for Christmas presents this year, because retailers jack up prices to allow for the money they expect to lose to the "return artists."

It Was the One-Armed Man—Really!

Arizona
December 2008

According to a news blog in Arizona, the employees at an electronics store had a television stolen from under their noses by a most unlikely burglar: a double amputee. Allegedly, the fellow entered the store with two accomplices. The accomplices strapped a 27-inch TV to the amputee's back, and he walked out completely unnoticed. Employees later discovered what had happened when they realized they were missing a TV. They went to the videotape and saw what had happened from the surveillance camera's point of view. No word on whether charges were pressed or the thief was arrested, but public opinion would probably err toward letting the guy keep his Christmastime steal as the reward for a pretty impressive swipe.

Surprise, You're on Christmas Candid Camera!

Lydd, England
December 2008

Bulbs, bulbs, bulbs! Every holiday season the tiny town of Lydd in Southeast England sees more and more bulbs disappear from the community tree. By 2008, Town Councillor Clive Goddard was sick of it. "Why should everyone suffer because of a few people?" he asked the local newspaper. Each year the vandals outdid themselves. In 2008, the tree had only been up for two weeks and already forty-five bulbs were missing. At the cost of roughly a pound each, the thievery was beginning to become a burden on taxpayers. After some debate, the town decided to invest in a security camera in time for the following year's holiday season, realizing it was a better investment to spend money on a camera than on countless missing bulbs in the future.

A Christmas Miracle?
Nope.

Baby Jesuses are stolen all over—it's not just a North American phenomenon. The cherub was kidnapped from a Nativity scene at a shopping mall called the Kwinana Hub in western Australia. An excitable shopper noticed Jesus was missing, and she stormed into the mall's management office demanding to know what had happened. They were just as surprised as she was. They posted a sign asking for the Baby Jesus to be returned, but to no avail. They suspected a local fellow who was known for his strong belief that no Baby Jesus should enter a Nativity scene until after Christmas Eve, but they couldn't prove it. The mall manager turned away people's offers of Barbie and Pamela Anderson dolls to replace Jesus, insisting the babe was bound to reappear. It was, after all, Christmas.

Skimming a Little Off the Top

Bristol, England
November 2002

During the holiday season of 2002, "skimmers" rushed to take advantage of as many innocent people as they could before the UK changed their credit cards over from a swipe-the-strip to a chip-and-pin system. *The Western Daily Press* in England reported that skimming was on the increase. This form of credit card fraud happens when shopkeepers and clerks steal customers' credit card info and pass it to gangs who use it to make counterfeit cards. The victim only realizes what has happened when they get their credit card statements. Authorities expected the chip-and-pin system, which requires the user to punch in a personal pin number as opposed to signing a receipt, to foil these scamming skimmers. But they also expected the holiday season to be a rough one as the unscrupulous folk realized it was their last chance.

Santa's Naughty List Just Keeps Getting Longer and Longer

London, England
December 1999

If you're going to make a career out of pick pocketing, you'd do best in a major city crowded with tourists and wallets plump with cash. It was hard not to think of the gang of pickpockets in the famous musical *Oliver!* when the *London Evening Standard* reported modern-day Artful Dodgers had descended upon the city for the 1999 holiday season. Normally about eight hundred pick pocketing incidents are reported per month, but that figure doubled in November 1999. (Merry Christmas, London!) The newspaper wrote that the upswing in dipping (English slang for pick pocketing) was due to the arrival of organized gangs from around the world—Kosovo, Bosnia, South America—who were stealing to the tune of £500–£1,000 per day (about $800–$1,600). Guard your pockets, everyone! Fagin would be proud.

A Well-Planned Christmas Caper

Christchurch, New Zealand
December 2000

On the Friday before Christmas, a very organized and savvy group of robbers stole more than $1 million from a security van parked in front of a historic building. Before setting the van and building on fire, they changed the lock on the building, ensuring that no one could get in—and by pulling off the heist the Friday before the holiday, they made it very hard for the police to track down witnesses. The plot was so well-coordinated, it could have made it's way to a Hollywood production. Finally, an example of a Christmas crime done well!

Save Yourself, Action Man!

Polhill, United Kingdom
December 2002

A gang of thieves stole a group of action figures from a Tesco store and were being chased by cops when they rolled down the windows and flung the loot to the ground to get rid of the evidence. Disappointingly, the action figures did not spring to action. They just lay there. Or did they? The police caught the crooks, but when they came back to claim the figures, they were gone. A policeman reached out to the figures' new owner in the paper, pleading, "If anyone did pick up some Action Man toys in the Polhill area, we would be very pleased if they could let us know." He went on to describe them as approximately one foot high.

They Must Have Stolen Santa's Sleigh to Get Up There

Kidderminster, United Kingdom
December 2007

Just a few days before Christmas, some thieves scrambled up to the roof of a parish church in an English town and stripped it of £5,000 worth of lead flashing (over $8,000). Lead must be worth a whole lot on the black market for them to risk life and limb that high up in the middle of the night—the crime happened between midnight and 9:30 in the morning. But the lead had incredible sentimental value for the churchgoers, and the reverend told the local paper she hoped there was enough evidence to catch the perpetrators, adding that most people in the community were imbued with the proper holiday spirit even if a criminal minority was "clearly just out for what they can take."

Because You Can't Ask Santa for a Carton of Smokes

Essex, England
November 2008

Police are well aware of the sorts of crime that tend to spike during the days leading up to Christmas. Among these are theft of alcohol and cigarettes. Partying is an important part of the holiday season, and these festive accoutrements are very much in demand. Still, they couldn't prevent two major raids from occurring in mid-November 2008. The first involved a Volvo truck and two trailers hauling away kegs and cases of lager in the middle of the night. In the second, three burglars wearing white masks used crowbars to break into a market at midnight. They stole £10,000 (nearly $16,000) of cigarettes. It's unknown whether the crews were the same, but if so, they were planning on having one hell of a party.

On the Twelfth Day of Christmas, a Policeman Gave to Me . . .

South Yorkshire, England
December 2006

The South Yorkshire authorities patted themselves on the back for a job well done when they enacted Operation Christmas Impact during a twelve-day period in December. It was a new twist on the classic Christmas carol "The Twelve Days of Christmas." ("On the twelfth day of Christmas, my policeman gave to me, a warrant to search my living room . . .") The Operation involved securing warrants to raid the homes of people with outstanding crimes or who were breaching court orders. The police turned up, among other illegalities, cannabis plants worth £6,000 (nearly $10,000); a wardrobe holding £15,000 (almost $25,000) in cash; and a young man and woman involved in undisclosed drug offenses. The chief constable told the newspaper, "We want to give law-abiding citizens a happy Christmas and criminals a depressing and miserable one."

Faking the Holiday Spirit

Vidalia, Mississippi
December 2008

The Concordia Christmas Charity Fund does not give away preprinted checks. It gives away toys, food, and gift cards. The fact that a young couple—a twenty-three-year-old woman and twenty-seven-year-old man—were trying to cash checks from the fund was a tip-off to authorities that something was amiss. The couple was arrested and police issued warrants for two more suspects who'd succeeded in cashing fake $500 checks. The sheriff alerted local businesses to be on the lookout for more scammers, and he told the local newspaper, "Area businesses have to be extremely cautious year-round, but particularly during the holiday season . . ." Luckily, most scammers aren't great fact-checkers or check-makers.

Some Holiday Sales Are Too Good to Be True

West Yorkshire, England
November 2008

Sales of fakes—fake designer clothing, shoes, accessories, etc.—is a big business around the holidays when people are shopping for gifts. Unfortunately, shoppers often fall for things that are too good to be true (like a $20 Rolex.) In West Yorkshire, a group of trading standards officers and trademark experts went on a three-day raid to find the people behind the fakes being sold around the region. As one trading standards officer told the local newspaper, counterfeits can be dangerous: The strong scent of a bottle of fake Chanel No. 5 is very likely due to an unsavory source: sewage-laced water. Fake vodka is often made of industrial alcohol, which can make someone go blind. And, the officer added, they've seized fake condoms that can very well lead to, er, accidents. After three days, they'd arrested four people, searched twenty-one premises, and questioned five people—but they weren't having any luck getting to the organized gangs behind the street vendors. Through the newspaper, they asked Christmas bargain hunters to cease and desist, pointing out that they were only fueling the fire.

Even Criminals Want to Be Home for the Holidays

**Seychelles Islands
September 2006**

You may have heard of "island time," the euphemism that expresses how time seems to move much, much more slowly when you're living on or visiting an island. People there are just more laid-back—must be something in the ocean air. That was certainly the case in the Seychelles Islands in 2006, when people being charged with crimes and their lawyers campaigned to delay their court dates until after Christmas. The whole stressful process was guaranteed to ruin their holidays, so why not wait until after December? The islands' chief judge told a reporter, "Why rush to prison when you can celebrate Christmas in freedom first?" Why, indeed? It seems like they should've delayed their crimes, too, if they were so determined to celebrate Christmas in freedom.

A Seasonal Setup

Cardiff, Wales
December 2008

What a setup! Welsh police launched a special initiative called Operation Panther that was as complex as it was successful. They staged several move-ins, complete with empty homes, moving crews to cart inside 42-inch televisions and boxes touting the presence of high-tech equipment, and fake "moms" to put up curtains in the windows. Four trap houses all worked like charms. Video cameras recorded teenage thieves as they broke into the houses and stole the loot. The initiative, meant as a deterrent to other burglars, resulted in a major drop in crime in that part of the city. One police detective involved in Operation Panther told the newspaper that their timing was intentional, as burglaries increase in the weeks leading up to Christmas: "Criminals know people have presents and other valuables at home," he said. It looks like the people of Cardiff will only have Santa breaking into their homes this holiday season.

Enough Christmas Hams
for an Army

Sydney, Australia
December 2007

Burglars are usually unapologetic scoundrels, but some can be rather polite. This was the case with some thieves who left a thank-you note in the wake of their destruction. The owner of a ham warehouse in Australia found a huge hole in the wall when he arrived at work Monday morning. He soon discovered the absence of sixteen metric tons of ham and bacon—it was a ham heist worth $100,000 Australian dollars (over $91,000). Scribbled on the wall was a note: "Thanks . . . Merry Christmas." The warehouse owner was not amused. Christmas is high season for ham. He offered a $5,000 reward for recovery of his merchandise and immediately got to work figuring out how to fill all of his Christmas orders.

Remember Furby Fever?

Los Angeles, California
December 1998

Every year there's a hot toy. It's the one that every kid must have and that every parent must procure for their kid—no matter what! In 1998, that toy was a Furby, the 6.5-inch tall, interactive, electronic robot. In LA, thieves went to the trouble of smashing the front window of a hobby store to snatch two Furbys right out of the display, leaving the rest of the store entirely intact. The stolen Furbys were worth $500 and $200, but the shop owner was glad to see them go. Now he wouldn't have to witness any more temper tantrums by kids who desperately wanted the creatures for Christmas. "It's a shame that people kind of lose perspective about what the holidays are all about," the spokeswoman for Furby told the newspaper. You have to wonder if she felt it was a shame when the earnings reports came in.

I'll Be Home Brewing for the Holidays

Queensland, Australia
December 2007

An unprecedented Christmas crime spree overtook a small island off the northeast coast of Australia after a man broke into a local tavern. When security officers confronted him, twelve other people showed up and bullied the officers into locking themselves in an office. They called for backup, and when those policemen arrived it had already been a long night for them, since they had to fly in from the mainland. They arrested eight people, ages twelve to thirty-four, for some obvious and some not so obvious crimes. Each was charged with one count of possessing home brew, an act that was made illegal on the island since an alcohol management plan was introduced a few years earlier. It's unclear whether the twelve-year-old was also imbibing the home brew.

Three Stolen Presents, Two Surprised Robbers, and a Parking Lot Vigilante

Concord, North Carolina
December 2005

A mall parking lot vigilante saved the day when a couple in North Carolina was mugged by two robbers lying in wait for departing shoppers. One mugger grabbed the woman's purse as the other pushed her husband to the ground and took the presents—an iPod, a digital camera, and clothing the couple had just bought for their grandchildren. Luckily, a fellow who had played defensive back for his college football team saw the whole thing go down from the safety of his car. He chased the robbers in his vehicle, then jumped out and tackled the one who was holding the packages. The two robbers, suitably intimidated by the man's heft and tackling skills, fled, leaving the grandkids' presents intact. Algebra may not come in very handy later in life, but playing football sure does.

Too Much Booty
for One Pair of Pants

Lapel, Indiana
December 2006

A teenager in Indiana was the victim of very poor planning—and Sir Isaac Newton's law of gravity—when she shoplifted more than her pants could handle. The store owner saw the teen pocket several items as she was making her way through the aisles, so he confronted her as she tried to leave. The police car was pulling up as she tried to run, and her pants, weighted down by all that booty, fell to her ankles, effectively doing the police's job and straitjacketing her so she couldn't flee. Found in her pockets were a potato peeler, an ice cream scoop, two cake decorating gel tubes, and six ROLO candy bars. She faced one count of (undeniable) theft.

Santa Sees You When You're Sleeping, and So Do the Police

West Yorkshire, England
December 2008

In merry old England, Christmas means Operation Christmas Crime Crunch. Authorities found that criminal activity often increased around Christmas, so to be proactive they created "rings of steel" around crime hotspots and sent a proliferation of uniformed officers and plainclothes detectives out and about on Christmas Eve. A few days before Christmas, they'd already arrested and charged twenty people, arrested and bailed thirty-four, and executed six warrants. The inspector in charge of the operation warned, "If you're a criminal, you better watch out, because we'll be watching you."

The Case of the Missing Icon

The owner of a coffee shop in Nashville arrived one morning around Christmastime to find his most famous cinnamon bun missing from its display case. The bun had first gained notoriety in 1996 when a customer pointed out how closely it resembled Mother Teresa. The observation drew attention from international news outlets, and the coffee shop owner preserved the bun in shellac for all eternity. He commissioned T-shirts, prayer cards, and mugs imprinted with an image of the bun until Mother Teresa, before her death in 1997, wrote to ask that the merchandising come to an end. The owner theorized that the thief really didn't like the display, as he went right for the bun and totally ignored the cash lying nearby.

Scrooges
& Grinches

ALWAYS Listen to Your Mother

Rock Hill, South Carolina
December 2006

What's a twelve-year-old to do in the face of a wrapped present lying in plain sight beneath his Christmas tree? It's the ultimate temptation. And despite his mother and his great-grandmother's warnings not to open the gift, one twelve-year-old in South Carolina just had to see what was inside. The boy's mother soon noticed that the gift was unwrapped and the box that once held a Nintendo Game Boy was empty. She accused the boy, but he denied it. When she threatened to call the police, he owned up to it and produced the toy. Mom called the police anyway. When the authorities arrived at the house, they arrested the twelve-year-old for petty larceny. It's not been reported whether he was allowed to bring his Game Boy with him to jail.

Not the Right Year to Sit at the Grown-Ups' Table

Franklin, Tennessee

A family squabble is most likely to escalate into a family brawl during the holidays, when different generations and sides of the family come together for a big, chaotic celebration. That was the story in Tennessee when a man insisted his son sit at the "grown-ups" table for their holiday dinner. The boy's grandma, and the evening's hostess, apparently had a different idea of what being a grown-up meant, because she angrily clocked her son-in-law, then threw a stereo at her grandson, injuring the poor kid. What ever happened to peace on earth, goodwill toward men?

They Didn't Like Santa's Taste

San Rafael, California
December 2004

It's the thought that counts. That's what Miss Manners says. She says to understand the motivation behind the gift—to remember that this person wants to please you and to honor your relationship with something they thought you'd like. A pair in California obviously didn't get this message because they had a wholly opposite reaction to receiving gifts they deemed unsatisfactory. After unwrapping their parcels, the two men smacked each other over the heads with flowerpots, leading to the hospitalization of both. Bah humbug.

The Christmas Chain Saw Massacre

Pontypool, South Wales
December 2001

An innocent Christmas-tree seller was asleep in his van at a roundabout in a small town in Great Britain when he was awoken by a very unpleasant surprise, namely a man with a chainsaw. This man was a rival tree seller and was seemingly determined to cut down his competition. The chainsaw wielder head-butted his rival, then took the saw to his trees, slicing them in half—bringing new meaning to the phrase "undercutting the competition." As of the next day, he still hadn't been caught by the police.

The Trojan Reindeer

World Wide Web
December 2006

If you got an e-mail with a subject line that read, "Merry Christmas to our hero sons and daughters" and came with an attachment called "Christmas+Blessing-4.ppt," would you open it? Many did in 2006 when the e-mail was circulating during the holiday season. They had no way of knowing that the file, once opened, would silently add two additional, malicious files to their computer. It was the feat of work-for-hire Chinese hackers, paid to mess with Western businesses by implanting dangerous office documents on their employees' computers. The name of this variety of hack? A "Trojan horse." Don't look it in the mouth. Don't open it.

When You Gotta Go, You Gotta Go

Taunton, Massachusetts
November 2006

It was a real Grinch who relieved himself on the holiday decorations adorning the church green of a small Massachusetts town. The town hadn't finished decorating for the holidays yet when the sixty-one-year-old man leaned against a veterans' statue, unzipped, and peed, managing to hit a tree, some holiday lights, and the statue in full view of cars and passersby. Despite the setback, the town planned to regroup and continue decorating. The director of their park and public grounds told the local paper, "There will be security when all the decorations are finally up."

What the Hell Is
a Holiday Tree?

Toronto, Ontario, Canada
November 2002

O nce upon a time in the city of Toronto, some very official officials decided to ban the word "Christmas" because of its lack of political correctness. How about the people who celebrate Hanukkah or Kwanzaa, they asked? Doesn't everyone pay taxes? Why should Christmas get all the attention at the exclusion of others? They decreed via a press release that the tree at City Hall would heretofore be called the Holiday Tree. Soon after, the mayor, who was Jewish, reversed their decree, restoring the moniker "Christmas tree" and introducing a bylaw that forbade the tree from being called by any other name.

Grinches across the Continent

Toronto, Canada; Washington; and Florida
December 2006

What do some people have against Christmas trees? A lot, it seems. One Toronto judge who oversees the Ontario Court of Justice ordered a small, artificial tree be removed from the courthouse because, or so she assumed, the Christian symbol might alienate people of other cultures and religions. Earlier that month, fourteen trees were removed forcibly from the Seattle-Tacoma International Airport when a local rabbi complained about the lack of a menorah in the same facility. And in Florida a landlord banned tenants from putting up Christmas decorations. All three acts met with significant public outcry and resulted in the reinstatement of the trees and decorations, showing once and for all that Christmas trees are above the law—or at least above the law as dictated by personal opinion.

Where Will They Hang Their Stockings Now?

New York, New York
December 1999

I t was just like a scene from *Rent*, the musical, except no one was singing. When a group of starving artists moved into an abandoned factory building in a desolate section of Brooklyn in the late 1980s, they never would've guessed at such a bleak ending. Over ten years, they'd transformed the space into a maze of small art studios and living spaces. They weren't living there legally, but they were relatively comfortable, and the rent was dirt cheap. No one bothered them until a few days before Christmas in 1999, when officials from New York City Department of Buildings forced them to leave their homes, claiming their squats were dangerous, even going so far as to claim they posed an "imminent danger to the safety and life" of the residents. Heavy padlocks were placed on doors as artists were thrown out into the cold with their easels, paints, and dishes. Some had nowhere else to go—nowhere else to celebrate Christmas. One artist complained to the *New York Times*, "My God, it's Christmas. This is criminal." Said a city spokesperson, "Safety takes no holidays."

No Whoville in Louisville

Louisville, Kentucky
November 2008

What the mayor knows about lawyers could fill a book—at least a Dr. Seuss book. "It appears these lawyers' hearts are two sizes too small," the Louisville mayor told the local newspaper after receiving a cease-and-desist letter from DLA Piper, the firm representing Dr. Seuss Enterprises. The crime? Using the village and characters from *How the Grinch Stole Christmas* as the basis for the town's annual Light Up Louisville celebration. Plans were in place to erect a "LouWhoVille," populated with Cindy Lou Who and the Grinch, when the letter threatening legal action arrived. The town had no choice but to quickly change course by taking the "who" out of "LouWhoVille" and renaming the display, "Lou-ville." It looks like this is a story where the Grinch *did* steal Christmas.

Sleigh Bells Ring,
Are You Blaspheming?

Rome, Italy
December 2007

Gold, frankincense, myrrh . . . and Red Bull? No way, said an angry Italian priest when he saw a commercial for the caffeinated drink that portrayed four wise men instead of three—the fourth bearing a can of Red Bull—visiting Jesus and Mary in Bethlehem. From his desk in Sicily, the priest wrote the company an angry missive, labeling the commercial "a blasphemous act" and calling it disrespectful to Christianity. The incident was not without precedent, as Italian priests had previously called for the removal of advertisements by clothing label Marithé et François Girbaud and notorious rock star Madonna. Red Bull promptly replied with a promise to remove the commercial. They didn't say whether they'd alter their slogan, which could also be interpreted as blasphemous: "Red Bull gives you wings."

Doesn't the NRA
Deserve an Ornament?

Philadelphia, Pennsylvania
November 2006

Urban Outfitters unveiled a highly controversial tree ornament—a glittery representation of a five-inch handgun on a satin ribbon—just in time for the holidays! And just in time to inadvertently raise the hackles of anti-gun and anti-violence groups. The groups called for the company to take the Glitter Gun Ornament off the shelves and to issue an apology.

It wasn't the first time the company courted controversy. They'd previously been taken to task for T-shirts that read, "Everyone Loves a Jewish Girl" and illustrated with a dollar sign, and "New Mexico: Cleaner than Regular Mexico." They may have drawn the most vocal ire for their board game called Ghettopoly, in which players compete to buy crack houses instead of Park Place and Boardwalk.

In response to the outrage over the Glitter Gun, the company issued a statement saying the ornament was by no means meant to condone or celebrate gun violence.

A Very Un-Merry Christmas

Pasadena, California
December 2004

What are you going to do if your kids are badly behaved on Christmas? Give them coal? How about not giving them any gifts at all? One Pasadena dad decided to take it a step further when he put the Nintendo DS video system plus three games that were intended for his three sons on eBay, so his kids could watch as others vied to win their precious holiday booty. Mom and Dad had warned their sons that if they didn't cut out the fighting, cussing, and obscene gestures, their gifts were going up on eBay. The boys promised to change their ways, but to no avail. As part of the product posting, Dad wrote, "No kidding. Three un-deserving boys have crossed the line. Tonight we sat down and showed them what they WILL NOT get for Christmas this year. I'll be taking the tree down tomorrow." Unfortunately, by the end of the auction, bids on the $700 worth of video games were only up to $465.01. The man said he'd post them again or return them, but there was no way they were going under the tree.

What a Freakin' Scrooge!

Novara, Italy
December 2008

A Catholic priest in northern Italy was bursting bubbles and killing illusions all over town by telling kids there was no such thing as Santa. His words stoked the anger of dozens of parents who claimed that the priest ruined their kids' Christmases. The priest defended himself by insisting he was only trying to educate kids on the difference between Jesus, who was real, and Santa, who is fictional—like Cinderella or Snow White. His logical explanation did nothing to calm the angry parents who would have preferred that their children's whimsy and innocence remained intact for a few more years.

Fruitcakes or Nut Cases?

Manitou Springs, Colorado
December 2007

You would think the annual Great Fruitcake Toss in Manitou Springs would be a pretty lax event. After all, it sounds kind of silly. But the organizers of the Toss have as many rules and regulations as an Olympics qualifying committee. For one, all fruitcakes are inspected by Fruitcake Toss Tech Inspectors to make sure the cake is an actual fruitcake made of glacéed fruit, nuts, and flour (and not inedible items that might make the cake easier to toss). The inspectors also look at weight—the cake must qualify for one of two classes: two pound or four pound. Lastly, no fruitcake launch device can be powered by fuel. (Pneumatic spud guns may be used but only in a separate, designated competition.) And if all that wasn't enough to worry about, showmanship is a factor in judging, too, with the crowd empowered to vote for "best entourage." Who knew something so wacky could be so high-pressured?

And You Thought Your Neighbor's Christmas Display Was Bad!

Indianapolis, Indiana
December 2006

When something irks you, you can take it to the Internet. There you're bound to find folks who are simpatico. That's what one Indianapolis homeowner supposed when she launched a Web site in 2006 called tackychristmasyards.com. Through the site, she urged people to send in pictures of especially tacky displays, even going so far as to provide a list of specific violation categories, including "more is not less," "multiple Clauses," and "fallen figurines," meaning displays in which some of the decorations have fallen over. As she wrote on the Web site, "No one wants to see Mary and Joseph laying [sic] down as if involved in a deadly drive-by shooting."

They Take Their Oversize Inflatable Christmas Scooby-Doo *Very* Seriously

Allen, Texas
December 2006

Neighborhood holiday display competitions are a growing phenomenon across the US, spurred on by the growing number of community associations who are always looking to do something to build community spirit, which in turn ups people's pride and property values. The number of associations grew from two hundred forty thousand in 2001 to three hundred thousand in 2006. The community in Allen really got into it, with displays that became more and more spectacular each year. Soon, oversize snow globes and Scooby-Doos were on the menu. To make sure there wasn't any funny business with the judging, they went so far as to bring in outsiders who were sure not to be swayed by any personal bias. Despite the general excitement, there were still those in the community who were bitten by the bah humbug. One woman told the newspaper she was turned off by all the lighted displays. "What ever happened to global warming?" she wondered. Instead of destroying the environment for her own personal gratification, she decided to contribute greenery and flags.

One Way to Fight the Winter Doldrums

Birr, Switzerland
December 2007

Something was not right in the picturesque Swiss town of Birr and the surrounding villages. People's Christmas decorations were being swiped, one by one, over the course of a few days. The bizarre crimes were a mystery until a couple of people out walking spied a forty-nine-year-old woman blatantly stealing Christmas decorations from someone's private garden and stashing them in her bag. They stopped her and called the police, who found almost $2,000 worth of illuminated reindeer, plastic snowmen, miniature figurines, and Christmas ornaments in the woman's house. The Grinch should move to Birr if he's ever looking for a wife.

The Great Christmas Carol Protest

Greencastle, Indiana
December 2005

Atown's efforts to be politically correct were met with sheer outrage when the city council voted to replace Christmas and Good Friday with more generic, all-encompassing names like "winter holiday" and "spring holiday." In response to the vote, hundreds of townspeople staged an unusual protest. They wielded carols in lieu of signs when they filled council's chambers and launched into a rousing rendition of "We Wish You a Merry Christmas." Less than a week after the policy was voted into practice, it was tidily—and merrily—reversed.

December
Disasters

A Christmas Present They'll Never Forget

Chaparral, New Mexico
December 2007

Ouch! Like it doesn't hurt enough to get a tattoo. Just before the holidays, two men in New Mexico were prepping to tattoo an image of a gun on one man's arm. To create the design, one held a .357 Magnum up to the other's skin and tried to trace its outline. Kids: Don't try this at home. The gun went off, hitting one in the hand and the other in the arm. Not the best Christmas presents they'd ever received, but certainly ones they would not forget.

Honey, Have You Seen the Carving Knife?

Rock Springs, Wyoming
December 2007

A few days before Christmas, a 9-1-1 center in Wyoming received an alarming call just after one A.M. The man on the line told them he'd just been stabbed in the chest—by his wife. She was very angry with him, and why wouldn't she be? He'd opened her Christmas present early. As with many couple's spats, this one turned out to be about something much larger—according to court records, the wife suspected her husband of having an affair. The two had only been married under four months before the wife was arrested and charged with assault and battery. Everyone says the first year of marriage is the hardest.

She Just Wanted to Be with Her Family for the Holidays—Even if They Were Imaginary

Miami, Florida
December 2008

Christmas stories should be populated with miracles, dancing sugarplums, and dashing reindeer—not a lying woman, a made-up baby, a fictional French nanny, and a distraught father. But when one Florida woman decided all she wanted for Christmas was to be reunited with her ex-boyfriend, she pretended she'd had his baby and the baby was missing. Telling her story over Christmas Eve and Christmas Day to anyone who would listen—including the local TV news—the sobbing woman claimed her six-month-old baby boy had disappeared with her French nanny, Camille.

The TV news shows flashed photos of an adorable infant. Police scrambled to find the cherub. So everyone was more than a little upset to find there was never a baby. She had done it all in an attempt to keep her ex-boyfriend interested. She told him she'd had a healthy baby boy. When the ex flew down from Boston to meet his progeny, she had to think fast. She bought baby clothes and tucked them into a dresser. She swiped baby photos off the Internet, and she made up the Camille story. The whole thing was a lie.

Some *Very* Special Christmas Brownies

South Bend, Indiana
December 2000

W hen the gift is off base, it's the thought that counts; but what about when the gift is dangerous and potentially injurious? That was the case in South Bend when a woman delivered brownies to local firefighters. The baked goods seemed like an innocent, thoughtful gift—a token of thanks to the men who keep the town safe and sound. But the firefighters who ate the brownies became ill—two required treatment at the hospital. It turns out the brownies were riddled with marijuana. The firefighters were neither expecting pot brownies nor were they fans of drug-laced desserts.

Some believed the special delivery was meant to make a statement about the board of safety refusing to dismiss a firefighter who'd twice tested positive for cocaine. The woman suspected of baking the brownies was charged with two felony counts of battery and two misdemeanor counts of criminal recklessness. The firefighters turned out to be fine—well, they were a little paranoid for a while.

Maybe He Really Hates Parades

**Anderson, South Carolina
December 2006**

Don't drink and drive. This is especially good advice when the vehicle you're driving is a float in the annual Christmas parade. Unfortunately, this advice was not followed in Anderson one Christmas, and the driver of a truck hauling a float belonging to a local dance studio recklessly sped past another float and ran a red light on Main Street. Police pursued him, but instead of pulling over, he took them on a three-mile chase. There were nineteen people—adults and children—on the float, including his own child. It turns out the driver had an open container of alcohol in his truck. According to the paper, he admitted to "bad judgment" at the ensuing court hearing.

You Have to See Him through His Mother's Eyes . . . That Is If You Can See Past the Wall of Fire

Brooklyn, New York
December 2000

You'd think that someone who sets aflame nineteen houses worth of holiday decorations must be a fan of fire. Not according to the mother of the twenty-year-old man charged and arrested for committing this act. "I can vouch with my life that he would never do anything with fire," she told the newspaper. "Graffiti maybe, but not fire." His mother could take solace in the fact that he wasn't prosecuted under the state's hate-crime laws. His arson was equally spread among secular (scarecrows and cornucopias) and Christmas (wreaths) décor. The Police Commissioner reported, "It wasn't anti-Christmas. It was sort of anti-everything."

Not Even Santa
Could Bring Home a Win

Philadelphia, Pennsylvania
December 1968

O h, those Philadelphia sports fans. They sure love their sports teams when they're winning, but when they're losing, they can turn faster than mayo in the sun. In 1968, more than fifty-four thousand people turned up to watch the Eagles play the final game of the season. Their record going into the game was 2-11 (two wins, eleven losses), and the weather was freezing. It'd been snowing steadily since the night before—fans had to scoop three inches of slush from their seats. The Eagles took a seven-point lead, but the Vikings tied the score at 7–7 just before halftime. Fans were already in a sour mood when the Christmas-themed halftime show began. For some reason, Santa hadn't made it to the stadium. In desperation, the director of the show plucked a man from the audience who was dressed in a fake beard and red corduroys to fill in for Saint Nick. Maybe because of the Eagles' losing season, or maybe because the man made a lame-looking Santa, the fans began pelting him with snowballs as he made his way around the field. The incident lives on as a symbol of the ruthlessness of Philadelphia's fans: They'll even boo (and attack) Santa Claus.

Fa-la-la-la-la-la-la-la-OUCH!

Clarksville, Tennessee
December 2003

His wife, he told the paper, insisted they have exterior lights on their house that year. She'd had them growing up, and she'd coveted them on her neighbors' homes, but she and her husband were always too busy with their small children to string their own house. This year was going to be different. The husband's parents came over to help babysit so he could hang the lights. Jokingly, he told them all before heading outside, "If you hear a loud bang, call 9-1-1." Famous last words.

Sure enough, the family heard a loud bang, and he was on the ground. He had slipped and fallen seventeen feet to the ground while he was hanging lights on the roof. Aside from a couple of hairline fractures and a chipped vertebra, he was fine. In her letter to Santa that year, his three-year-old daughter asked for "my daddy to get better." Her mother told the local paper, "Never again. Next year we'll just go for lights in the yard."

For When You Don't Have the Time to Look Like You Care

London, England
December 2008

Imagine being hired because you do something extraordinarily poorly. That is sort of the case with several employees of the gift Web site Firebox.com for their new service called CrapWrap. The idea: to professionally wrap presents so badly, they look like they may have actually been wrapped by your boyfriend or husband. You know, the one who's all thumbs. The service costs $5.90 and is performed by the company's warehouse workers and truck drivers. A spokesperson reported that the same number of people who were asking for skilled wrapping for their holiday orders were requesting the crappy wrapping option. "Women like to think that their husbands and boyfriends took the trouble to wrap the present themselves," she surmised, "even if they made an appalling hash of it."

I'm Getting Roadkill
for Christmas

London, England
November 2007

What kid wouldn't want a cuddly teddy bear for Christmas? What kid wouldn't want a cuddly teddy bear with his eyes popped out, guts spilling over, and an ID tag attached to his toe explaining his cause of death? That's the question people had to ask when news broke before Christmas 2007 of an English toy company, Compost Communications, launching a line of roadkill plush toys. A spokesperson for the company advised that the toys were not suitable for individuals who are easily upset—or did he mean nauseated?

The first toy in the line was Twitch, a raccoon who'd met a tragic end. Twitch came with a transparent body bag "to keep the maggots out." Already on the assembly line were Twitch's buddies Grind the rabbit, Splodge the hedgehog, and Pop the weasel. Each priced at approximately $50, they reaffirm the notion that one man's trash is another man's treasure.

I'll Have Seconds
on the Irony, Please

Lawrenceville, Illinois
December 2008

What happens at the office Christmas party stays at the office Christmas party—unless the party is thrown by the county health department and the scandal is food poisoning. That's impossible to keep quiet. The irony is just too rich. That's why a local paper reported that the Lawrence County Health Department held a buffet for seventy-two people, and forty-two of them, including the department head, got sick to their stomachs. The culprit was contaminated food. The department head suspected the cold diced ham in the salad bar. Or, she suggested, "It may be that a food handler was sick at the time and handled some of the food they prepped for the meal." All together now: Eeeeeew! In addition to feeling sick to her stomach, she was feeling sick over the situation: "I'm telling you, it got me down. I about passed out and everything else," she said. "It's not been funny." Oh, but we beg to differ.

Oy Vey!

New York, New York
December 2007

You would think Balducci's, a grocery store that caters to a high-end clientele, would know better. It's located in the sophisticated, worldly metropolis of New York City. Still, someone made a huge mistake by posting signs advertising ham with the following hook: "Delicious for Chanukah." D'oh! Many Jewish people keep kosher all year, meaning they follow a list of dietary laws that dictate, among other things, that no pork or other pig products can be consumed, but almost *all* Jews eat kosher for Chanukah.

Word got out after a woman took photos of the signs and posted them on her blog. When asked to comment, the store's director of marketing informed the Associated Press that the signs were changed immediately, and that the company would be reviewing its employee training.

'Tis the Septic Season

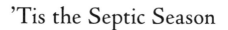

Really? Did it have to happen this way? And if it was going to happen at all, did it have to be on Christmas Eve? One seventy-seven-year-old man had a very stinky holiday in 2007 when he went outside to do some work on the clogged septic tank. Unfortunately, he fell through the tank's access door headfirst and got stuck. He hung in there, wedged in the door, for an entire hour before his wife finally looked out the window and saw the poor man's legs kicking in the air. (Or at least that's her story.) She called 9-1-1 and the authorities came to release the man from his scatological nightmare.

Now Who Will Pull Santa's Sleigh?

Franklin Park, Pennsylvania
December 2001

A deer hunter in Pennsylvania "popped a cap" in a reindeer the day before Christmas, shooting and killing the unfortunate, semi-mythical beast at close range. The reindeer and one of its friends had escaped from a Christmas display in a nearby town. One reindeer was captured, but the other escaped into the woods—the last place you want to be during deer-hunting season in western Pennsylvania (an area sometimes referred to as "Pennsyltucky"). As there was no law in the books forbidding people from hunting reindeer, the hunter faced no charges. He just felt really guilty when he had to go home and explain to his kids why he'd taken down Dasher.

Unhappy
Holidays

There Aren't Just Presents
Hidden in the Attic

Wilkes-Barre, Pennsylvania
December 2008

As the saying goes, "Houseguests are like fish: They stink after three days." Maybe that is why a twenty-one-year-old man was asked by friends to leave their Pennsylvania home one December. Apparently he had no place to go, because instead of leaving via the front door, he left through a trapdoor in an attic that was shared with the neighboring duplex. The man made his home in the attic, making jaunts into the house below whenever he needed food. He also helped himself to clothing, cash, and Christmas presents, keeping track of all the loot on a list he labeled his "Christmas List." The woman who owned the duplex smelled something fishy as soon as she began to realize things were missing and—this clinched it—when she spotted footprints on the floor of her closet where the attic trapdoor was located. She called the police. Finding him was, well, kind of like shooting fish in a barrel.

She *Really* Wanted a New Kitchen for Christmas

East Dene, England
December 2007

Renovating can be a real bummer. Dealing with contractors going over budget and over schedule is no fun, especially around the holidays when bad things can be blown out of proportion due to the season's added stress. According to the London Sun, a great-grandmother of two in Northern England got *so* frustrated with her contractors, she barricaded her door and threatened to imprison two home improvement workers and two supervisors until they were finished remodeling her kitchen. The workers called the police on their cell phones, and the authorities showed up at the house with a battering ram. A local mediator ended up working out a compromise through the letter box as the great-granny explained she was not going to hurt the workers, she just wanted to make a point. "They have had me up nearly every day at 6:00 A.M. for them to start at 8:00 A.M. and then they didn't turn up," she told the paper. "I just couldn't take it any more."

Dimmer than a Burned-Out Christmas Bulb

Baltimore, Maryland
December 2008

Emotions can run high around the holidays, and no one is more emotive than a die-hard sports fan whose team isn't performing. One Baltimore Ravens fan was so distressed over his team's poor showing that he climbed to the roof of a local tavern on December 11 and remained there until Christmas Day to draw attention to his grief over the suckiness of his football team. Little did he know (although he may have guessed if he'd stopped to think about it) that the stunt would backfire in a huge way. As he carried on for the local press about the money he'd spent on team memorabilia and on his own personal anguish, his ex-wife saw the coverage and rejoiced in finding him after looking for years to recoup the $40,000 he owed her in child support. She wasn't the only one. Later, another woman stepped up to the plate to claim the $12,000 the disgruntled sports fan owed *her* in child support. It's safe to say he soon had much more to protest than the poor performance of his Ravens.

Ho-Ho-Hoax

Lafayette, Colorado
December 2004

A man in Lafayette fooled the world when he rigged an elaborate hoax convincing people they could control the seventeen thousand Christmas lights on his property via his Web site. He claimed he'd written computer code that allowed visitors to his site to virtually control different zones in his elaborate system of lights. Local media picked up the story. Then the Associated Press sent news of the cyber-controlled lights around the nation. A local news station took the man up in their helicopter so he could explain to viewers how it was possible to turn certain sections on and off via the Web.

The news coverage brought more than one million people to his site, but the ruse was up after a few weeks when a *Wall Street Journal* reporter started investigating and the man admitted that the whole thing had been a trick. He later apologized on his Web site to people who were angered by his trickery, claiming it was all in good fun and his intent was to "bring joy and a smile to people's faces."

Better Navigation Skills than a Wise Man

Atlanta, Georgia
October 2008

An Atlanta family was devastated when they came home from a holiday vacation to Mexico and found that Pepper, the beloved golden retriever they'd had for five years, had disappeared. On Christmas! That counts as a negative gift. The dog-sitter told them the dog had been startled and run away when someone started setting off firecrackers nearby. After a few months passed, the owners had to accept that Pepper was gone, and they adopted another golden retriever. But Pepper's owners had had a microchip embedded in his neck, so when the owner of a Tampa Bay–area travel agency found the very neglected-looking dog and brought him to a veterinarian, they were able to track down Pepper's parents. Somehow Pepper had traveled five hundred miles in nine months, and no one will ever know how, but his return was surely a post-Christmas miracle. And when he returned to Atlanta, he had a gift of his own: a new sibling.

It's Sort of Like Getting a Christmas Bonus

Wallingford, Connecticut
January 1997

Wallingford is not a city that's apt to bend the rules, not even over the holidays. Let's just say, no one would accuse them of being softies. Case and point: A city employee, a woman in her seventies, took it upon herself to trim the city's Christmas tree during the Thanksgiving holiday. Was their response a Christmas bonus? An extra vacation day? A Best Buy gift card? Nope, it was a one-day unpaid suspension from work. The reason? It's illegal to be in the building after hours. Here's hoping she spent her day off looking for a new gig.

Assault with a
Deadly Decoration

Victoria, British Columbia
December 2004

It's a classic battle of the sexes story . . . or is it? It's the holiday season, and a man and a woman are on their way home after a day of shopping. She's carrying the Christmas tree they just purchased, and he's carrying bags of gifts. He makes a comment that the gifts are heavier than the tree. She gets upset. *Verrry* upset. So upset that she takes the tree and beats him with it. And not just a love tap, either; she beats him with the tree so much that she ends up in handcuffs! Okay, so it's a classic battle of the sexes story gone haywire.

Hate Thy Neighbors

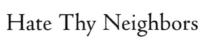

Jensen Beach, Florida
December 2004

Hooray and yay for the Florida woman who won the Christmas lights competition in her apartment complex! Good for her. Er, good for her until a losing neighbor became enraged and ripped out her winning display. Some people can't stand losing, even when it's a contest of holiday spirits. Add another check mark against humanity and a new type of rage to the fast-growing list: holiday contest rage.

Well, the Holidays Are Supposed to Be a Time of Sharing

Tarpon Springs, Florida
January 2004

Never believe what you read, including classified ads for rental properties in Florida in the winter. That might be the lesson to learn from this anecdote of a man in his forties who collected money in advance for renting out his mobile home outside of Tampa. He collected money from at least nineteen people who were expecting to rent his home starting January 1. Come New Year's Day, the renters began showing up, but they found the man still living in his home. He had no intention of leaving. The sheriff arrested and charged him with defrauding the northerners for a total of $33,000. Law enforcement told the local paper, "I don't think he thought too much about what would happen when everybody showed up."

Maybe These Days
It's Cheaper than Coal

Cambridgeshire, England
December 2006

Britain's Peterborough prison made news around the holidays in 2006 for throwing a party for their inmates. There's nothing especially newsworthy about a party, but this one featured Xboxes and PlayStations and cash gifts of £5 each (to spend on what is not clear). The trouble was, these cash gifts were higher in value than the candy boxes gifted to the jail's guards. Of course, the guards still had their freedom. It was questionable, this question of value.

An Uncommon Holiday Venture

Murfreesboro, Tennessee
December 2007

One thing you don't want around the holidays is a neighbor whose house is emitting all kinds of nasty smells. That's just the kind of snafu that might ruin the ambience at your annual holiday party. Maybe that's why some people in Murfreesboro complained to the police in December 2007 about a specific house in their neighborhood. When police raided the place, they found and confiscated 114 deceased cats and one dog. They could not have guessed that the owner of the dead animals would then slap them with a $1.5 million lawsuit claiming the carcasses were "business property." Apparently he was planning to open a pet cemetery and needed some dead pets to get that venture going. In his petition to the court, he also wrote that one of the cats was exceptional because it had been so large at birth.

Some People Are Really Difficult to Shop For

Portsmouth, New Hampshire
December 2008

Who doesn't want a Wii for Christmas? One twenty-six-year-old man in New Hampshire, that's who. And he let his grandparents know how much he didn't want one. After they gave him one for Christmas, the ungrateful grandson blew his top, complaining that what he'd really wanted was a remote-controlled airplane.

His girlfriend couldn't stand his juvenile behavior, so she told him to cut it out. He redirected his anger toward her, and the couple got in a scuffle that included him dragging her down the stairs by her hair and her punching him in the eye. It's unclear what the grandparents were doing while all this transpired—perhaps playing with the Wii? The couple was arrested on charges of domestic-related simple assault.

Cards for Convicts

South Wales
December 2006

It's not the merriest Christmas card to receive: the front shows a prisoner lying on a mattress in a cell next to a tiny Christmas tree and a toilet. On the front it reads: "Happy Christmas?" And on the inside: "Where are you going to spend Christmas day? Season's Greetings from South Wales Police," and the signature of the detective superintendent. The card, sent to 680 rapists and pedophiles in the district, was meant as a clear-cut reminder: The police are ever-vigilant, even over the holidays. One of the card's recipients told the local paper he thought the cards were a waste of taxpayers' money and in "extraordinarily bad taste."

Oh Christmas Tree, Oh Christmas Tree, How Dangerous Are Thy Branches

**Manatee County, Florida
December 2008**

We may be nearing the era when Christmas trees, like most everything that's sold these days, come with this disclaimer: a Christmas tree is not a weapon. When did this symbol of a joyous holiday—of families coming together and singing of peace, joy, and holy babies—turn into a sort of spear? Sometimes, to be fair, you get angry and it's the only thing around. This must've been what happened in 2008 when a man in Manatee County became enraged with his father, picked up the tree, and threw it at dad. He was later charged with felony assault.

Merry Cannabis!

Grove, Oklahoma
December 2006

It's kind of sweet that an Oklahoma woman brought her jailed boyfriend a Christmas card hiding a holiday treat: marijuana. It probably wasn't the best plan, however, to bring an illegal substance into a county jail. And the story loses its sweetness when you discover why the boyfriend was in jail in the first place: for repeatedly ramming his girlfriend's car. Too bad they both ended up in jail with no marijuana or even a Christmas fruitcake.

Merry Christmas, Everybody
(Except Slade)

Kensington, England
December 2008

The powers that be at a Holiday Inn in London banned a popular Christmas tune when too many guests complained. The song in question—"Merry Christmas Everybody" by Slade—was a UK hit in 1973, making it to the *Top of the Pops*. Apparently people in 2008 don't share the tastes of the previous generation. A local paper called it "the only song to have been withdrawn by public demand," and a hotel spokeswoman assured, "If there are any more Christmas turkeys that guests want to ban, we will be listening out for any serious requests."

I Want a Hippopotamus
for Christmas

Vancouver, British Columbia, Canada
December 2005

I t's important to be kind to all creatures—including hippos—around the holidays. A zoo outside of Vancouver learned this the hard way when they were slapped with charges of cruelty to animals for keeping their two-year-old hippo, Hazina, alone in a windowless shed in a pool so shallow she couldn't float. When they acquired Hazina in October 2004 they promised to build her a new home, but in June authorities said their time was up: They were taking too long. A spokesperson for the local humane society also criticized the zoo for hiring out Hazina to a company called TELUS for a Christmastime TV commercial to promote their high-speed Internet service. When TELUS heard of the controversy, it insisted the entirety of the hippo's $10,000 fee go toward paying for her new, spacious home.

Santa, Big Brother, and Everyone on Your Block Are Watching

Aberdeenshire, Scotland
December 2003

Nosy neighbors everywhere rejoiced when police in Scotland encouraged their curtain-peeking ways by handing out two thousand notepads, instructing people to write down reports of suspicious behavior. The authorities launched "Operation Big Brother" in the weeks leading up to Christmas, as they expected crime to spike as it does every year. This joyous season goes hand-in-hand with criminals breaking into houses and cars, hoping to pilfer expensive, unused presents, or so the cops explained. The initiative (i.e., the notepads) was funded by neighborhood watch groups, which begs the question—don't most people have an extra notepad or two lying around? Better peek in their windows and check.

Justice Clearly Doesn't Take a Christmas Vacation

Christchurch, New Zealand
December 2008

Two weeks before Christmas, more than one hundred police got up early, put on their stab-resistant body armor, and fanned out across the city to arrest up to 730 people who had outstanding warrants. They wanted to ensure they'd be caught before they had the chance to wreak holiday havoc. By late morning, the courthouse was overflowing. By the end of the day, more than two hundred offenders had been dragged in, most with warrants for failing to appear in court. A sergeant told the newspaper they were hoping to send a clear message. That message was clearly not "Happy holidays."

1 Mad Russian + 1 Crazed American x Scottish Whisky = Big Trouble

Allentown, Pennsylvania
January 2004

If you think there's going to be trouble when you've got two guys with nicknames like "Crazy Eddie" and "the Mad Russian," you're right. In January 2004, the two got in an argument and, according to the police, Crazy Eddie fired a sawed-off shotgun at his friend. So not cool! But the two men, who lived across the street from one another and both drove tractor-trailers, later insisted no such thing had occurred. Yes, there was a sawed-off shotgun, and yes, it was fired—but it was an accident, they claimed. They'd been celebrating Orthodox Christmas and drinking "Scottish whisky." In fact, they denied everything, including their nicknames. When a county judge asked the Mad Russian, "So, you're the Mad Russian?" the man replied, in a heavy Slavic accent, "I'm not Russian, and I'm not mad."

Hand-Delivered
Holiday Wishes

Staffordshire, England
December 2007

The English are so polite, aren't they? They even send Christmas cards to criminals, or at least the police do. But the policemen's cards tend not to be filled with cheer: In 2007, the Staffordshire police custom-ordered cards that pictured a battering ram on the front, and inside the card read, "We have our own ways of opening doors this Christmas. We are targeting known criminals who want other people to pay for their Christmas." The police visited anybody who was convicted or even suspected of committing burglary in the past to deliver this special sentiment. Do not expect Hallmark to pick the card up for general distribution anytime soon.

A Not-So-Tasty Christmas Cracker

Wellington, New Zealand
December 2007

Christmas crackers are a lovely holiday tradition throughout the Western world. The shiny columns are often filled with treats and surprises like fortunes, paper hats, and riddles. When you pull on either end, the cracker makes one loud *crack!* and all of its contents spill out. Families usually open them at the holiday table. One woman in New Zealand got a not-so-pleasant surprise in her cracker when she cracked it open and found a dead mouse. The woman told her local newspaper that in hindsight she smelled something funny and couldn't discern the source. She recalled remarking as much to her granddaughter. All was revealed when the mouse tumbled out and her niece reached for it, thinking it was a toy. The newspaper that reported the story was unable to reach the Indonesian manufacturer for comment.

A New Use for a Christmas Classic

Chattanooga, Tennessee
December 2008

The afterlife of Christmas trees—who knew they were destined to swim with the fishes? In Tennessee, fishermen and the wildlife agency officers troll Lowe's and The Home Depot on December 26 for leftover evergreens. The stores donate the trees to be used to create fish habitats beneath docks in fishing areas. The fish are drawn to the network of underwater crevices created by the submerged trees.

But the practice has grown competitive—on the day after Christmas, wildlife agency officers have to beat the local fishermen to the tree stores, because fishermen want to claim the trees for their own favorite fishing spots. There should be enough to go around—an estimated 150 to 200 trees per year are repurposed as holiday gifts for the fish. Or is it more of a gift for the fishermen?

I Think I'd Prefer Myrrh

Nazareth, Israel
December 2008

As souvenirs go, postcards, T-shirts, and key chains can get really old, really fast. One enterprising merchant in a small village near Nazareth came up with a much more unusual idea for a souvenir: He sealed donkey dung in transparent plastic boxes. Call it "Holy Crap," or, if you prefer, "Holy Land Crap." As donkeys are part of the Nativity story that takes place in this area of the world, bringing home a piece of their poop is just like bringing home a piece of the age-old story. Albeit a piece of the story they never mention in the Bible. Worse yet, there is no easy way to determine whether the poop was actually from a donkey . . .

Maybe He Just Wanted a Nice Picture for His Christmas Cards

Los Angeles, California
December 2008

A few weeks before Christmas, a probation officer busted an eighteen-year-old gang member for violating an injunction order that forbade him from seeing his fellow gang members. During a routine visit to the gang member's home, the officer noticed a key chain decorated with a photo of the man and three guys in his gang posing with a nearby mall Santa Claus. Apparently Santa was a big enough draw to get him to do something entirely illegal, as he wasn't permitted to sit, stand, or gather with other gang members in a 1.4 square mile safety zone. (No word on whether the injunction included a ban on posing with Santa.) For his visit with Jolly Saint Nick, the eighteen-year-old was looking at eighteen months in jail, which would mean no temptation to go see Santa the following holiday season.

Brighter than the North Star

Little Rock, Arkansas
December 1993

The time the Christmas display on steroids blew a transformer and darkened the streets—that was the talk of the town. Then again, this particular Christmas display was probably the subject of conversation every year. After all, it's something that can probably be seen from the moon. With 1.6 million lights, computerized snow, wise men, and sleighing Santas, the couple who puts up the display is using enough juice that a spokesperson from the local Arkansas Power & Light Company estimated their December bill at $1,000. He surmised they must use as much electricity in December as the average home in their neighborhood consumes in an entire year. Maybe this is why they were hauled into court on charges of being a public nuisance and found themselves, one holiday season, defending their show in front of a judge instead of presiding over the extravaganza that they insisted was meant as a gift to their neighbors.

Like Jews for Jesus, but with More Lights

Los Angeles, California
December 2006

People will do exactly what they want to do, no matter what other people think. That's certainly the case in one largely Orthodox Jewish neighborhood in Los Angeles where one Jewish family mounts an exuberant Christmas display every year, complete with fake snow, giant snow globes attached to the roof, and some larger-than-life Santas. The matriarch of the family explained to a reporter that her family has had holiday displays since she was a little girl. Why would she stop a tradition? Still, a lot of the neighbors, including the Israeli neighbor across the street, didn't understand. According to other neighbors, he yelled at her, "What kind of Jewish girl puts a Santa in the yard?" Probably the kind of Jewish girl who thinks Santa can be fun for anyone of any creed.

They Don't Give Games Names Like *Trouble* for Nothing

London, England
December 2006

Some targeted studies released in 2006 provided a unique look at family holiday dynamics in the United Kingdom. A good number of arguments are caused by disagreements over which presents to open. Then there are the old standby arguments—those old differences that flare up whenever the whole family gets together. One in five family arguments is caused by a disagreement over what to watch on TV. More people argue over what to watch than argue over who's washing up after dinner. But there's something that trumps both: board games, which cause arguments in twenty-four percent of households. People should know by now not to let grandma be the banker—she always cheats!

A Ten Thousand–Watt Christmas

Redding, California
December 2006

Christmastime 2006 was a banner year for holiday decorations. Sales were up nine percent from 2004 with people spending $500 million on inflatable ornaments. This was life before the Great Recession. Unfortunately, not everyone was a fan of blow-up holiday spectacles. One fellow in California upset his neighbors with his twenty-eight-foot lighted arch, fifty-foot tree, and dozens of animated silhouettes. His display attracted busloads of tourists who clogged the streets and threw their trash on the neighbors' lawns. The Christmas music also kept his neighbors awake. They complained to authorities, who informed the festive fellow he'd have to get a special events permit and remove the large containers he used to store all those props the rest of the year. His neighbors ended up causing him so much strife that he ultimately opted to put an end to the annual display. A city group saved the day when they asked him to set up his lights and figurines downtown to draw people into the city. "I think the one who was happiest was my wife," he admitted to a local paper. "She was getting tired of people looking in our windows."

This Was Definitely Not on Rudolph's Wish List

Cape Town, South Africa
December 2002

A reindeer in a Christmas display in a South African shopping mall lost his manhood after spectators complained about the inappropriateness of the gold, shiny balls dangling between his hind legs. The company who set up the display told a local reporter that the balls were "anatomically correct" for a reindeer of that size, presumably unaware that the point of a Christmas display is to evoke cheer rather than to give kids an education in the size of a grown reindeer's genitalia. A mall manager castrated the creature so as not to continue to alarm his customers. After all, there were plenty of other malls in town whose holiday displays did not cross the line between PG and X-rated.

It's Christmas All Year Long for Mary

Gainesville, Georgia
December 2005

Learning the name of one Georgia woman, Mary Theresa Christmas, prompts several reactions. They might include, "At least it isn't 'Seymour Butts,'" or, "What were her parents thinking?" Who knows, maybe her parents couldn't predict how many corny "Have a Mary Christmas" jokes she'd have to endure. Ms. Christmas told one local newspaper that people often think she's playing a prank. Some store clerks will even call fellow clerks over to gape at her ID. With all this in mind, she is a phenomenally good sport, a true embodiment of the spirit of Christmas. "Even though they are one in a line of thousands," she told the paper, "they don't know that so I let them have their fun."

So That's Where the Holiday Traffic Starts!

Deerfield Township, Ohio
December 2005

You've heard of sun delay and gawker delay, also known as rubbernecking, but have you heard about Christmas-lights delay, or the occasional car accidents caused by holiday displays? Luckily no one was hurt in one such accident in Ohio, where two cars crashed when the drivers were distracted by an eccentric light show. This display cost $10,000, used twenty-five thousand Christmas lights, and took two months to set up. The lights were synched by a computer to music that was beamed to car radios. The twelve-minute show consisted of three songs, including "God Bless the USA" and "Wizards in Winter." After the accident, police couldn't get to the vehicles because of all the cars lined up to watch the show. The homeowner, an electrical engineer, immediately turned it off, saying he'd told police from the beginning that if his lights caused any traffic snarls, he'd be more than happy to shut it down.

It Seemed Like a Good Idea at the Time

Westminster, Colorado
December 2006

A Colorado man who'd locked himself out of his house had apparently seen too many holiday movies. His solution was to try to break into his own home through his chimney. Apparently he'd missed the "do not try this at home" message, as he got stuck somewhere inside the twelve-foot-high tunnel and had to be rescued by firefighters bearing ladders in the wee hours of the morning. The lesson: Unless you're a stunt person, Santa Claus, or beanpole-thin, stay away from the chimney.